Praise for

Depth Takes a Holiday

"A master of the excruciating moment. She is very, very funny . . . She has a gift for showing us just how stupid our stupid lives really are."   —T. Coraghessan Boyle

"All the pieces are terrific: intimate, acerbic . . . and really, really funny. Less like . . . an essay collection and more like . . . a long, fabulous phone conversation with a witty, insightful pal."   —*Entertainment Weekly*

"In these days, when the short humorous essay has de-volved to a plodding reminiscence leading up to a rickety punchline, a passel of puns, or a romp through the the-saurus, Tsing Loh's pieces have an electric crackle and a stink of L.A. smog that put *The New Yorker* back page in its place."

    —Daniel Pinkwater, author of *The Afterlife Diet*

"Tsing Loh [is] a wisecracking literary cousin to Merrill Markoe and Carrie Fisher . . . a sharp, earthy observer of an eccentric world."   —*Kirkus Reviews*

"A wonderfully funny writer. You will like her so much that you will be tempted to put her book inside your body. Don't. Remain decorous. Simply bask in the honeyed light of the Sandra afterglow."

    —Henry Alford, author of *Municipal Bondage*

continued . . .

"Cool, quick, trend-conscious and ironic . . . [she has] an unerring eye for where to stick the needle that punctures social pretensions." —*Toronto Globe and Mail*

"Just when you thought life wasn't all that funny anymore, along comes Sandra Tsing Loh. She's here to cheer us up." —*Arizona Daily Star*

"Insightful and hilarious . . . She's a natural commentator with an acute eye and a talent for humor. *Depth Takes a Holiday* would be a great book to take to the beach." —*Toronto Star*

"Funny, wonderfully mean and suspiciously wise." —*San Diego Union-Tribune*

"If Oscar Wilde could be brought back to life and persuaded to visit Los Angeles with Hunter Thompson as his guide, one wonders if even he could do justice to the place (justice being a malleable concept, as any Angelino can tell you) the way Sandra Tsing Loh has in this collection of essays. Hers is monster talent; this book represents the appearance of a seemingly inexhaustible source of tooth-gnashing discouragement to the rest of us, who must try (and usually fail) to be witty. Even her acknowledgments left me begging for mercy; don't read this book in a place where you are expected to keep quiet." —Mark Salzman, author of *Iron* and *Silk*

"She's funny, urban and self-deprecating. She's a wicked cultural observer given to sarcastic one-liners. She's jaded— and proud of it. Dorothy Parker? Fran Lebowitz? Nora Ephron? Well, no. Her name is Sandra Tsing Loh. You may not know the name yet, but chances are that you will. She's that good." —*Buffalo News*

Aliens in America

•   •

Sandra Tsing Loh

Riverhead Books, New York

Special thanks to *Quarterly West* ("My Father's Chinese Wives") and *Icarus* ("Sugar Plum Fairy"), in which the short stories upon which these monologues are based originally appeared.

Riverhead Books
Published by The Berkley Publishing Group
A member of Penguin Putnam Inc.
200 Madison Avenue
New York, New York 10016

First edition: September 1997

The Putnam Berkley World Wide Web site address is
http://www.berkley.com

Library of Congress Cataloging-in-Publication Data

Loh, Sandra Tsing.
   Aliens in America / Sandra Tsing Loh.—1st ed.
      p.   cm.
   ISBN 1-57322-627-0
   1. Parent and child—United States—Drama.   2. Parent and child—
United States—Humor.   3. Chinese American families—Drama.
4. Chinese   American   families—Humor.   5. Chinese   Americans—
Drama.   6. Chinese Americans—Humor.   7. Monologues.   I. Title.
PS3562.0459A79   1997
812'.54—dc21   96-54622
                                                                   CIP

Printed in the United States of America

10   9   8   7   6   5   4   3   2   1

Acknowledgments

Getting a one-person show to New York is a twofold miracle. On the one hand, the performer's history is rewritten in one stroke, the shining phrase "Off-Broadway production" supplanting the vastly more descriptive "decade-long trail of tears in which I lost a lot of money and spent years developing the wrong act entirely." Even more remarkable, though, is the miracle of collaboration and friendship any theatre piece represents. To the following people then I am most grateful . . .

Equity-waiver heroes of Los Angeles:
Jeff Murray and Nicolette Chaffey of Theatre/Theater
Dan Kwong of Highways
Adrienne Hampton and Susan J. Sullivan of
Theatre East
Eric Trules of Solo/LA

Brilliant creative minds who helped shape *Aliens in America*:
John Rechy
Tom Bryant
Brian Brophy
Stuart Ross

Acknowledgments

Key people who said "yes" along the way:
Robert Koehler and Don Shirley of the
Los Angeles Times
Eden Collinsworth of *Buzz*, and Mitch Douglas
at ICM
Kathrin King Segal of the HBO New Writers Project
Annie Albrecht and Bob Reed of the HBO Workspace
Stuart Smiley of the U.S. Comedy Arts Festival
in Aspen
Ira Glass of NPR's "This American Life"
Dinitia Smith of *The New York Times*

Providers of artistic sustenance, strong liquor, fatty snacks, comfy pillows and (when needed) apple potpourri:
The MacDowell Colony
Jessica Yu
Susan Marder
Adam Shulman of APA
Absolut Mary South

And most of all, the home team in New York:
Carole Rothman, and all the bright lights of Second
Stage Theatre—quite frankly, I love you (sniffle)
My wonderful director Steve Kaplan, true patron saint
of the theatre, a man of hand-wringing, yellow legal
pads, and midnight subway rides, without whom
the production would not have been possible.

For the Loh family: my father, Eugene Sr., my sister, Tatjana, my brother, Eugene Jr., and of course Gisela Jacobsen, the one we miss most of all

Aliens in America

1992

ADULTHOOD:

My Father's

Chinese Wives

My Father, the Alien

My father has decided—ten years after my mother's death, without the benefit of consulting either me or my sister—to take a Chinese wife.

He has written his family in Shanghai, seeking their help in locating likely candidates. He has good confidence in this project. He hopes to be married within six months.

Let us unpeel this news one layer at a time.

Question:

Is my father even what one would consider *mar-riageable* at this point?

At age seventy, my father—a retired Chinese aerospace engineer—is starting to look more and more like somebody's gardener. His feet shuffle along the patio in their broken sandals. He stoops to pull out one or two stray weeds, coughing phlegmatically. Later, he sits in a rattan chair and eats leathery green vegetables in brown sauce, his old eyes slitted wearily.

He is the sort of person one would refer to as "Old Dragon Whiskers." And not just because it's a picturesque Oriental way of speaking.

At times my father seems to be overacting this lizardy old part. "I am old now," he'll say with a certain studied poignance. "I am just your crazy old Chinese father."

If he's that old, why does he still do the same vigorous daily exercise regime he's done for the past twenty-five years—forty-five minutes of pull-ups, something that looks like the twist, and much unfocused bellowing? All this done on the most public beaches possible, in his favorite Speedo—one he found in a Dumpster.

No. "Crazy old Chinese father" is actually a kind of code word for the fact that my father has always had a hard time . . . spending money. Why buy a leather briefcase to take to work, goes the rap, when this empty Frosted Flakes cereal box will do just as well? Papers slip down neatly inside, pens can be clipped conveniently on either side.

Why buy Bounty paper towels when, at work, my father can just walk down the hallway to the men's washroom, open the dispenser, and lift out a stack? They're free—he can bring home as many as we want!

When you've worn a sweater for so long that the elbows have worn right through, just turn it around! Wear it backwards! Clip a bowtie on—no one will notice!

Why drive the car to work when you can take the so-convenient RTD bus? More time to read interesting scientific papers . . . and here they are, in my empty Frosted Flakes box!

"Oh . . . terrific!" is my older sister Kaitlin's response when I phone her with the news. Bear in mind that Kaitlin has not seen my father in ten years, preferring to nurse her bad memories of him independently, via a therapist. She allows herself a laugh, laying aside her customary dull hostility for a moment of more jocular hostility. "And who does he think would want to marry *him*?"

"Someone Chinese," I say.

"Oh good! That narrows down the field to what? Half a billion? No, as always, he's doing this to punish us.

"Think about it," she continues with her usual chilling logic. "He marries a German woman the first time around. It's a disaster. You and I symbolize that. It's a disaster because he's passive-aggressive, he's cheap, and he's angry. But of course he won't see it that way. To him, it will have been that rebellious Aryan strain that's the problem.

"You take an Asian immigrant just off the boat, on the other hand. Here is a woman fleeing a life of oppression under a Communist government and no public sanitation and working in a bicycle factory for ten cents an hour and repeated floggings every hour on the hour, every day of every week of every month of every year. After that, living with our father might seem like just another bizarre incident of some kind."

As usual, Kaitlin scores some compelling points, but I'm bothered for yet a different reason . . .

Because in describing this potential new wife, my father has used one word: Chinese. He has not said: "I'm looking for a smart wife," or even "a fat wife." He has said "Chinese." That word is meant to stand for so much.

Asian. Asian women. Young Asian *ladies*.

I think back to a writing workshop I once attended. (No credit, and perhaps that was appropriate.) The students consisted of thirteen hysterical women—and one Fred. Fred was a wealthy Caucasian sixtysomething urologist who always insisted on holding the door open for me. Just for me. "Because you're such a lovely lady," he'd say—even as I stood there, literally, in glasses and sweatpants.

We thirteen women, on the other hand, were a wildly mixed group. We were writing anything from wintery Ann Beattie-esque snippets to sci-fi romance/porn novels (aka: "She would be King Zenothar's concubine whether she liked it or not"). We attacked each other's writing accordingly. People were bursting into tears every week, then making up as we emotionally shared stories about mutual eating disorders.

But there was one moment where all thirteen of us were of like minds. It was the moment when Fred would enter the classroom, laden with Xeroxes, blushing shyly as a new bride. We'd look at each other in horror as if to say: "Oh my God. Fred has brought in work again."

As though springing from a murky, bottomless well, each week new chapters would appear from this semi-epistolary novel Fred was penning about a wealthy Caucasian sixtysomething urologist (named Fred) who goes on sabbatical for a year to Japan. There he finds unexpected love in the form of a twenty-three-year-old Japanese medical student named Aku who smells of cherry blossoms.

There were many awkward scenes in which Fred and Aku were exploring each other's bodies as they lay—as far as I could gather—upon the bare floor, only a *tatami* mat for comfort. (Fred would always italicize the Japanese words, as if to separate and somehow protect them from the other, lesser words.) But it was all much more beautiful and much more pure than anything any of us could imagine, totally unlike the urban squalor of America—the rock music, the drugs, the uncouth teenagers!

But there's one line I've never been able to blot from my mind. Nor the way Fred read it, in that hoarse, tremulous voice.

"I put my hand in hers, and her little fingers opened like the petals of a moist flower."

It is a month later. As if in a dream, I sit with my father at the worn Formica family dining room table, photos and letters spread out before us.

Since my father has written to Shanghai, the mail has come pouring in. I have to face the fact that my father is, well, hot.

"You see?" he says. "Seven women have written! Ha!" He beams, his gold molar glinting. He drinks steaming green tea from a chipped laboratory beaker, which he handles with a "Beauty and the Beast" potholder.

With a sigh, I turn to the matter at hand. And in spite of myself, I am wowed!

Tzau Pa, Ling Ling, Sui Pai . . . The names jump off the pages in both their English and Chinese translations. While totally Asian, these are not retiring Madame Butterfly types.

"Twenty-eight, administrative assistant!" "Forty-nine, owner of a seamstress business!" "Thirty-seven, freelance beautician!" These women are dynamos, with black curly hair, in turtlenecks, jauntily riding bicycles, seated squarely on canons before military museums, beaming proudly with three grown daughters.

One thing unites them: They're all ready to leap off the mainland at the drop of a hat.

And don't think their careers and hobbies are going to keep them from being terrific wives. Quite the opposite. Several have excellent experience, including one who's been married twice already. The seamstress has sent him shorts and several pairs of socks; there is much talk of seven-course meals and ironing and terrific expertise in gardening.

Super-achievement, in short, is a major theme that applies to all! But the biggest star of all, of course, will be my father. He gleefully hands me a letter written by one Liu Tzun. It reads:

Dr. Loh,

Your family has told me of your excellent scientific genius and your many awards. I respect academic scholarship very highly, and would be honored to meet you on your next visit.

"You see? They have respect for me in China! When I go there, they treat me like President Bush. Free meals, free drinks! I do not pay for anything!"

Forty-seven-year-old Liu Tzun—the writer of the magic letter—is indeed the lucky winner. Within three months, she is flown to Los Angeles. She and my father are married a week later.

I do not get to meet her right away, but my father fills me in on the stats. And I have to confess, I'm surprised at how urban she is, how modern. Liu Tzun is a divorcee with, well, with ambitions in the entertainment business. Although she speaks no English, she seems to be an expert on American culture. The fact that Los Angeles is near Hollywood has not escaped her.

This is made clear to me one Sunday evening, via telephone.

"I know you have friends in the entertainment business," my father declares. He has never fully grasped the fact that most of the people I know do, like, hair for "America's Most Wanted."

"So you should know that, aside from having re-paired my shoes and being very skilled at Chinese folk dance, Liu Tzun is an excellent singer—"

"I'm sure Liu is quite accomplished. It's just that—"

"Oh . . . she is terrific!" My father is shocked that I could be calling Liu's musical talent into ques-tion. "Do you want to hear her sing? I will put her on the phone right now!"

"Oh my God. Don't humiliate her. Has it ever occurred to you that this singing is something that you want her to do, not that she wants to do? Like with my piano lessons as a kid? When you used to push me to the piano, push me to the piano, push me to the piano, and I'd cry, and you'd push me and I'd cry—"

But my father has not heard a word of it. He is too busy hustling new talent. I hear the clunking sound of two extensions being picked up.

"Okay, okay: she will sing for you now!"

"Hallooo!" a third voice trills—and I realize that, unlike me, Liu Tzun is not afraid to perform for my father. There is a professional clearing of the throat, and then:

"Nee-ee hoo-oo mau, tieh-hen see bau-hau jioo . . . !"

I have left you, Dr. Loh, and taken the Toyota—so there!

This is the note my father finds on the worn Formica family dining room table five weeks later. Apparently Liu's career was not moving quickly enough, so she left him to marry someone higher up—perhaps Ted Koppel.

My father is in shock. Then again, he is philosophical.

"That Liu—she was bad that one, bah! She says I do not buy her gifts. She says I do not like to go out at night. And it is true, I do not. But I say: 'Go!

See your friends in Chinatown. It is okay with me!'
I like it better when she leaves the house sometimes,
it is more quiet.

"But Liu does not want to take the bus. She
wants to drive the car! But you know me, I am your
. . . crazy old Chinese father. I don't want to pay for
her auto insurance."

And then he actually says, "As with many Asians,
Liu Tzun is a very bad driver."

"Ha!" is Kaitlin's only response. "Isn't it interesting how he seems to repell even his own kind."

Summer turns to fall in southern California, causing
the palm trees to sway a bit. The divorce is soon final,
Liu's prizes including $10,000, the microwave and
the Toyota.

Never one to dwell, my father has soon picked a
new bride: one Zhou Ping, thirty-seven, homemaker
from Qang-Zhou province! I groan.

"But no . . . Zhou Ping is very good. She comes

very highly recommended, not, I have to say, like that Liu. She was bad, that one, bah! Zhou Ping is very sensible and hardworking. She has had a tough life. Boy! She worked in a coal mine in Manchuria until she was twenty-five years old. The winters there were very, very bitter! She had to make her own shoes and clothing. Then she worked on a farming collective, where she raised cattle and several different kinds of crops—by herself! Corn, rice, beans, lichees—"

"I'm sure Zhou Ping is going to fit in really, really well in Los Angeles," I reply.

But Zhou Ping is indeed full of surprises. The news comes, to my surprise, from Kaitlin.

"I received . . . a *birthday card*. From Papa . . . and *Zhou Ping*. On the cover there is a clown holding balloons. It's from Hallmark. Inside in gold lettering, cursive, it says, 'Happy Birthday! Love, Zhou Ping and your *daddy*.' "

"Your what?"

"This is obviously Zhou Ping's handiwork. The envelope is not addressed in his handwriting. She clearly doesn't know that he doesn't give birthday cards. Especially not to *me*."

But a week later, Kaitlin receives birthday gifts in the mail: a box of "mooncakes," a bunch of orchids, and a sweater hand knit by Zhou Ping. "Oh no! Now I really have to call her. She clearly has no friends in America. He really picked someone he can walk all over this time. I think it's sad."

Kaitlin finally does call, catching Zhou Ping at an hour when my father is on the beach doing his exercises. And in spite of her broken English, Zhou Ping manages to convince Kaitlin to come home with me for a visit!

It will be Kaitlin's first trip home since our mother's death. And my first meeting of either of my father's two Chinese wives.

We pull up the familiar driveway in my Geo. Neither of us say a word. We peer out the windows.

The yard . . . doesn't look too bad. There are new sprinklers, and a kind of intricate irrigation system made of ingeniously placed rain gutters. New saplings have been planted. Enormous bundles of weeds flank the porch as if for some momentous occasion.

We ring the doorbell.

The door opens and a short, somewhat plump Chinese woman, in round glasses and a perfect bowl haircut, beams at us. She is wearing a bright yellow "I hate housework!" apron that my mother was once given as a gag gift—and I think never wore.

"Kat-lin! Sand-wa!" she exclaims in what seems like authentic joy. She is laughing and almost crying with emotion. "Wel-come home!" Then to Kaitlin, a shadow falling over her face: "I am so glad you finally come home to see your daddy. He old now."

As if exhausted by that moment of solemnity, Zhou Ping collapses into giggles. "Hoo-hoo-hoo! My English is no good, no good!"

Kaitlin's expression strains between joy and nausea. I jump in nervously: "Oh, it's nice to finally meet you!" "How do you like L.A.?" "What's that I smell from the kitchen? Is that Szechuan food? Or Mandarin? Or what province is that—?"

My father materializes from behind a potted plant. He is wearing a new handknit sweater and oddly formal dress pants. His gaze is fixed at a point on the floor.

"Long time no see!" he says to the point on the floor.

"Yes!" Kaitlin sings back, defiant, a kind of Winged Vengeance in perfect beige Anne Klein II leisurewear. "It certainly is!"

My father stands stiffly.

Kaitlin blazes.

"Well," he concludes. "It is good to see you."

Feeling, perhaps, that we should leave well enough alone, the Loh family, such as we are, continues on through the house. It is ablaze with color—in those sorts of eye-popping combinations you associate with Thai restaurants and Hindu shrines. There are big purple couches, peach rugs, and shiny brass trellises with creeping charlies everywhere.

All this redecorating came at no great expense, however.

"Do you see this rug?" my father points proudly. "Zhou Ping found it! In a Dumpster! They were going to throw it away!"

"Throw it away! See? It very nice!"

Over their heads, Kaitlin mouths one silent word at me: "Help."

My father trundles off to put music on his . . . brand-new CD player? "That bad Liu made me buy it!" he says. "Bah! But it is very nice."

"Dinner will be ready—in five minute!" Zhou Ping is off in a blaze of yellow.

21

Kaitlin grabs me by the arm, pulls me into the bathroom, slams the door. "This is so weird!"

We have not stood together in this bathroom in some fifteen years. It seems somehow different. The wallpaper is faded, the towels are new . . .

"Look," I say, "there in the corner. It's Mama's favorite framed etching of Leonardo da Vinci's *Praying Hands*."

"But look," Kaitlin says, "right next to it. Is that a glossy 'Bank of Canton' calendar from which a zaftig Asian female chortles?

"Look what he's making her do!" Kaitlin begins to pace, veins stand out on her temples. "Look what he's making her do! Can't he give the woman a decorating budget? This is a man who has $300,000 in mutual funds alone! Can't he liberate fifty of it to spend on a throw rug? I mean, I know things were really, really, really difficult in Shanghai but he hasn't lived there now for forty years, has he? Will it never end? Will it never end?"

"We'll eat, and then we'll leave" is my soothing mantra. "We'll eat, and then we'll leave. Twenty minutes. We'll be out on the freeway. Driving. Wind in our hair. Radio on. It'll all be behind us. And I promise, we'll never have to come back again."

Dinner is an authentic Chinese meal: chicken, shrimp, and egg dishes twirl before us. Steam is rising. Plates are passing. Rachmaninoff drifts in from the CD player. It almost resembles a meal any normal family would be having at this hour.

To see my father sitting at this familiar table with his new Chinese wife is to see something surprisingly . . . natural. In common rhythm they eat deftly with chopsticks—which Kaitlin and I fumble with—and converse quietly in Mandarin—not a word of which we can understand.

And I realize: it's not Zhou Ping who's the stranger at this table. It's Kaitlin and I. They are the same culture. We are not.

But Zhou Ping will have none of it. Hardy Manchurian builder that she is, she is determined to use the crude two-by-fours of her broken English to forge a rickety rope bridge between us.

"And you, Sand-wa! You play the piano, no? Mo-sart: he very nice. You will show me! And you, Katlin, you, you are a teacher, no? That is good, Katlin, good! Good. You, Katlin, you are very, very . . . good!"

My father puts his spoon down. He is chewing slowly, a frown growing. "This meat . . . is very, very greasy. Bah! I tell you not to buy this meat, Zhou Ping, I tell you not to buy this meat!"

There is a familiar rhythm to his words, gestures, expressions. And I realize that while one character may be new, this is the same dinner table, the same family, the same drama.

And the only question is, What will she do this time? Will she throw her napkin down, burst into tears, run from the room? Will she knock the table over, sending sauces splattering, crockery breaking? Will we hear the car engine turn over from the garage as she flees into the night, leaving us here, frightened and panicked?

But Zhou Ping does none of these things.

She tilts her head back, her eyes crinkle . . . and laughter pours out of her, peal after peal after peal. It is a big laugh, an enormous laugh, the laugh of a woman who has birthed calves and hoed crops and seen winters decimate entire countrysides.

She points to our father and says words that sound incredible to our ears:

"You papa—he so funny!"

And suddenly my father is laughing! And I am laughing!

But Kaitlin is not laughing.

"Why were you always so angry?"

My father just shrugs his shoulders.

"Oh no no no no no. Why could you never let the tiniest thing go? How could you do that to our family?"

And I realize that my father doesn't have an answer. It is as though rage were a chemical that reacted on him for twenty years and now, like a spirit, it has left him. And he's just old now. He is old.

Dusk falls, throwing long blue shadows across the worn parquet of the dining room floor. After a moment, my father asks Zhou Ping to sing a song. And she does so, simply. He translates:

> From the four corners of the earth
>
> My lover comes to me
>
> Playing the lute
>
> Like the wind over the water

He recites the words without embarrassment. And why shouldn't he? The song has nothing to do with him personally. It is from some old Chinese fable that's been passed down from generation to generation. It has to do with missing something, someone, some place maybe you can't even define anymore.

As Zhou Ping sings, everyone longs for home.

But what home? Zhou Ping, for her bitter winters? My father, for the Shanghai he left forty years ago? And what about Kaitlin and me? We are sitting in our own childhood home, and still we long for it.

1969

CHILDHOOD:

Ethiopian

Vacation

My Mother, the Alien

M y mother was an optimist. No I mean *really* an optimist. This was a woman who, in 1969, planned a family summer vacation ... to Ethiopia!

Granted, Ethiopia was not her first choice. Given her druthers, she would have hopped on a luxury ocean liner to Hawaii while young men in tight pants served her peach schnapps on a silver tray.

"Peach schnapps—it is the *most* elegant drink!" she'd tell us girls. My mother stood 5 foot 11, a fast-talking German brunette given to wearing bright red lipstick, big amber beads, polka-dot dresses. Kaitlin and I thought she was the most elegant person *we'd* ever seen. Then again, we were ages nine and six, respectively.

"Peach schnapps—we used to drink it all the time in Danzig, before the war, when your tante Thea und I used to waltz to Strauss's 'Blue Danube,' sankyouverymach, at the glittering ballroom in Sopport built right over the sea. *Mit ro-o-osen gardenin!* And you know your mother's dance card was never empty in those days. There was Hans Heinlich, Karl Obst, Dieter Fischer-Kucher. Oh! Swarming like bees to honey!

"*What* is the perfume you are wearing? It is magnificent! What is it—Chanel No. 5? At least! Here, smell mine. It is called the Seralgio. You know what it is, a Seralgio? A harem! But you know what, I think I like yours better than mine! Is that possible? But I think so, because—"

My mother was a nonstop talker. She would not stop talking. That's why she was so sure her Hawaii pitch would work—"Palm trees, pineapples . . . Bali Hai! Bali Hai, Bali Hai, Bali Hai!"

My father was not impressed.

"It is not that I do not like to spend money. Oh no. Spend, spend, spend—that is all I do! It is just that I do not like to spend it on nothing."

Hawaii of course was nothing—a horror of sunny beaches, fruity drinks, laughing, happy people. Why would we want to go there? "Where is the education?"

My father, by contrast, was fascinated with places like Uzbekistan—where he'd wanted to go the previous summer. Why? Because he had a friend there we could stay with for free! But it was more than that.

"The people of Uzbekistan are very, very sensible and hardworking! They have had a tough life. Boy! The agrarian farm workers face a fascinating challenge with the tractors and combines that we will see at the science and technology museum blah blah blah blah . . ."

At this point, you might be wondering how two such opposite people as my parents got together in the first place.

I blame it on Buick. When my mother first saw my father, on that magical day in the mid '50s, he was sitting behind the wheel of a brand-new 1956 Buick. I guess a man looks better than he ought, in a Buick. Especially when it's surrounded by southern California in the '50s, a palm-fringed, swimming pool–dotted utopia lit by a sun so bright you actually start to hallucinate.

You believe you are in fact quite similar to a person.

#1. Both of you are new immigrants, recently escaped from bad circumstances in your home countries. My father was orphaned by age twelve in Shanghai, lived in poverty. My mother went through World War II, ran from soldiers, heard bombs drop around her.

Of course, my mother hated stories of some grim Zola-esque realism! Her favorite after-dinner stories were either goofy or schmaltzy, ending hopefully with a glass of peach schnapps and a sing-along of some kind. When American friends at dinner parties would ask her about hardship in Danzig, World War II, the Polish occupation, she'd cut them off at the pass.

"But enough of me. We are all of us travellers, *nicht va*? Foreign people in a foreign land. Und we all miss home, *nicht? Ja, ja. Prost!* Let us sing . . .

" 'Edelweiss! Edelweiss! Every morning you greet me!' "

Similarity #2 between my parents?————?

Nothing!

Except, I guess, that both had come to America—the place where miserable yesterdays could be traded in for joyous visions of tomorrow. And why not? It was the '60s. America was a great place to live! Jackie O. was in the White House, Apollo rockets were in the sky, the future was made flesh at eye-popping World's Fairs featuring whizzing monorails above, below, pavilions of happy, dancing Third World people joining hands and singing:

"It's a small world after all! It's a small world after all!"

So what if my parents had absolutely nothing in common! My mother would make this work! She would smush polar opposites together and invent something wonderful and new . . . like a raspberry linzer tort with sweet-and-sour hoisin frosting.

The first confident product of my parents' Sino-Germanic experiment was Kaitlin and I. Looking vaguely Hispanic, we were given Chinese middle names and hustled off to kindergarten in Heidi of the

Alps-type dirndls and clogs. We had more strange appendages grafted onto us than the jackalope.

Fashion victims of my mother's vision of a brave new (*wildly* cross-cultural) world, we were understandably suspicious of the idea of a family vacation in . . . Ethiopia.

"Ethiopia?" My father, of course, was immediately interested. And why not? Ethiopia was notoriously backward, wretched, poor. At that time too they were recovering from some sort of bloody civil war, leaving its countryside bleak, its peoples desperate. No one in the world would want to vacation there . . . which our father saw could be turned to our advantage.

"After all, if no one else is going, think how far the American dollar will go!"

"He thinks a vacation should cost one dollar! He's cheap—and mean!" we twin jackalopes, wary antlers trembling, pled to my mom. "He just doesn't want us to have fun. We don't *want* to go to Ethiopia!"

"Ethiopia? Where is that? Oh! You mean . . . Ethi-i-i-opia!" My mother sang it as though it were a Rodgers and Hammerstein musical, like "Oklahoma!" "Ethi-i-i-opia! Home of the magical town of Malawa—called the 'Pearl of the Red Sea'—with its byoooootiful beaches? Und its luxooorious resort hotel with its glittering ballroom built right over the sea, *mit ro-o-osen gardenin*, just like in Sopport?"

"Really?"

"Natürlich! It's right here in my *kleine Deutsche reise-buch*. Of course, your father doesn't know yet. He'll probably be quite angry. But once we get there, we will run away from your father, and swimonthebeach!"

"Yay!"

Air Ethiopia was not a good airline.

A plunging, four-hour ride on a shuddering gray

plane brought us to a town with the suspiciously gay name of Lalibella! "Lalibella!" my mother exclaimed in mock dismay as its airport—a manure field—rose up to meet us.

The "Hotel Lalibella" seemed made entirely of peat—and peat which had taken its kicks and beatings from the desert wind for a long time. Thick woven carpets with ominous symbols hung everywhere, exuding a faint hay smell. Kaitlin and I were given sour glasses of lemonade to drink as we perched on the family suitcases, watching sheep graze outside a big picture window.

All at once, the sheep screamed and scattered: a man in a galabiya was running after them with an axe!

I opened my mouth to let out a scream of terror when suddenly I heard my mother . . . *laugh*. What?

But indeed, there stood my mother with four German tourists, large and blond and gleaming in their sweat-streaked khaki, expensive cameras, and voluptuous leather travel bags draped around them like fresh kill. Apparently there was no place in Africa so miserable some German tourist did not want to take a photo of it.

"So *putzelinchens*!" my mother said. "You see: everyone's going to Malawa! Ilsa, Franz-Joseph, Friedl-Beums . . . *Hier sint mein tochters*—Kaitlin und Zandra. Zandra! *Nicht mit den nase*! Euuh! Euuh! *Und das ist mein mann*, Herr Professor Doctor Loh, *die kleine Chinezische*—"

With a wave of my mother's hand, soon the whole group was sitting down to a surprisingly festive Ethiopian dinner of bread and peas and potatoes. And, of course, fresh mutton that Kaitlin and I had watched nibble its last blades of grass a few hours earlier.

The adult buzz was growing to a roar. "Hoo-hoo-hoo-hoo!" There was much slapping of thighs and lifting of glasses. Even my father was having fun:

Franz-Joseph had just announced he was picking up the dinner tab. "*Du ferrukten Deutschen*!" my father guffawed in his terrible German, reaching over to goose Ilsa on the rear. Ilsa was big-hearted enough to laugh it off: I think the Germans were amused by my Chinese father as though he were a small attack dog.

But even as they were drinking, my mother knew that something was kaput. Which was that while the Germans were indeed headed to Malawa in the morning, they were planning to fly.

My father, of course, had just gotten tickets for the Bus.

Although back at the Addis Ababa Airport, I seemed to recall there had been some question of *safety* about the Bus. Never fully explained. "Please," one travel official in a shabby blue suit had pled with my parents. "You are wealthy Americans. The people of the Bus, they are *not good*."

But my father stood firm. Why ride in a plane for an hour when you could sit on a Bus for nine . . . and save almost $20! For four people.

"Besides, we are not stupid tourists. We will go the way the natives go! It will be so much more . . . educational."

But of course our German friends were not going to stand for that. So my mother had to fudge the truth . . . a little.

"But have you *heard* about the fabulous Bus?" she asked our friends over that festive Ethiopian dinner. Actually it was my mother who looked fabulous that evening: her crisp dark hair set off by a fire-engine red dress and big amber beads. "The scenery is absolutely stunning! You will miss it all by plane. Please! *Everyone* takes the Bus! It is what is done. Perhaps a bit on the rustic side, but *sehr gemütlich* in its own way. It is the one place where Adventure . . . and Economy . . . meet!

"Oh, my friends: you must take the Bus. Because we are all of us travellers, *nicht va?* Foreign people in a foreign land. And we all miss home, *nicht? Ja, ja. Prost!*

"Let us sing . . .

" 'Edelweiss! Edelweiss! You look happy to meet me!' "

So the mood is bright—if somewhat hung over—the next morning, when we all reconnoiter at the Bus "station"—yet another manure field.

"Güten Morgen!" my mother calls out.

"Güten Morgen!" the Germans call back. They supervise as a small Ethiopian hefts their fabulous leather luggage on top of the Bus, tying it all down with skeins of twine. The many Ethiopian peasants, the women in black muslin, the men in work shirts and wrinkled corduroys, pretty much ignore us, busy hefting their chicken coops and lentil baskets.

"A small detail," as my mother would like to put it later. "A small detail" is that there is not one, but two Buses heading out for Malawa this day. We and the Germans are all put together on the First Bus. Our family is further sub-divided into three seats at the front—ours—and one way, way at the back among the chicken coop's—my dad's. Good!

But here's the wrinkle. Our seats are right over the wheel. It rises in a hump under the floor. You can't stretch your legs out. For nine hours. And, as I've told you, my mother is 5 foot 11.

But the Bus officials do not want us to change our seats. Why? Because the First Bus is totally full. As for the Second Bus—for some reason, they do not want to put us on the Second Bus.

But my mother insists. She is on fire: the Pearl of the Red Sea is so close she can almost taste it. And so, over their protests, she marches us off to the Second Bus, far from anyone we know. Alone among . . . Ethiopians.

The Buses navigate down treacherous mountains. They are beautiful—if threatening—in their jagged blueness.

Occasionally a small child in soiled galabiya runs by the road, waving. His shout fades off in the distance: "Aaaaaaah!" The road zigzags, zigzags. At the end of each hairpin turn is a lone white cross. I drop off to sleep.

A popping—like the sound of a truck back-firing—jolts me awake.

All around us, Ethiopians are dropping to the floor. There is shouting outside. And then all at once, like a congregation, they rise and begin to file down the aisle, their fingers laced on top of heads.

My mother does not say two words to us; she kneels swiftly; her hands fly over our bags. She stuffs the family passports and traveller's checks under

Kaitlin's and my blouses, smoothing our waistbands to hold them in place . . .

"Are we there yet?" I ask. "What's going—?"

My mother claps her hand over my mouth and pushes me forward. When I get to the front door, I see what you get when Adventure . . . and Economy . . . meet: Eritrean terrorists clad in worn military fatigues, firing machine guns randomly into the air. Ahead of us, an Ethiopian peasant woman's cheap black purse is cut from her arm. Obedient as Ethiopian sheep, we file down the stairs and arrange ourselves along the side of the road into what seems, sickeningly, to be firing squad formation!

All around us is the blankness of the Eritrean desert. Ahead of us, the road to Malawa stretches out, pitted and empty.

"Oh my God," I think. "Oh my God."

I look over at my mother. But like us, her fingers

are laced on top of her head. And I realize, this is it. The end of my life. No more sour lemonade, no hay smell. I will never grow up to be nineteen. I will never get to see a glittering ballroom built right over the sea.

We wait. But the bullets do not come.

It gradually dawns on us that the terrorists' real interest is in the First Bus, not the Second. Indeed, fifty yards up the road, Ilsa, Franz-Joseph and the Fat Couple have become the center of attention. They stand helplessly in their sumptuous safari outfits, hands in the air, while the terrorist leader shouts at them.

My gaze slides down the line of First Bus terro- rees . . .

And there, near the end, is my father. With his small body, dark coloring, and worn rag sweater, he actually kind of . . . blends in. And I realize, with a kind of savvy world traveler's instinct, that my father will not be shot that day. And in spite of myself, I am glad.

Our German friends, on the other hand, are being marched toward the low brown hills as hostages.

"Ethi-i-iopia!"

It is five years later. In the safety of my parents' living room in southern California, my mother is concluding the Pearl of the Red Sea story for yet another group of mesmerized dinner guests.

"But Gisela!" someone asks. "How did you—? What did—?"

"But *natürlich*: the bus company set it all up! It was totally corrupt! They put all the foreigners on the First Bus to make it easy! Had it not been for the wheel, the wheel, I and the *putzelinchens* would have been marched off as hostages also! Our German friends were released two weeks later. But their passports, cameras, traveller's checks—they never got back . . .

"At that point, they may had wished they had flown. But then they would have missed all that stunning scenery!

"But . . . who needed to see the Pearl of the Red Sea anyway? Not us. That night, we dined on hot dogs and chocolate milk at the American Military Base in Malawa. We slept on metal beds. It was *so* elegant! *Morgan früh*, we were chauffeured straight back to Lalibella via military convoy. Which was fine with me, I said. As long as I don't have to . . . *sit over the wheel!*"

Everyone applauds and laughs, and so do I, wanting the story to go on and on.

But as the years go by, my mother gets more and more tired of telling it.

Because the Ethiopian vacation becomes the story of her marriage—a compromise between two opposites that can never be made to work. Eventually, my parents spend all their time alone screaming and fighting. Then they stop talking at all, living together in silence, two strangers under one roof.

But . . .

What my mother will do, sometimes, after a dinner party, is slip into the garage by herself. Still in her fire-engine red dress and big amber beads, she'll sit in the Buick, turn the radio on, smoke a cigarette.

Because the true mirage turned out to be not the Pearl of the Red Sea, but that Buick. When my mother had first seen it, in that magical day in the mid '50s, it was the car of a true-blue American, a man who had truly put his miserable past behind.

But that Buick turned out to be an anomaly in my father's life, a youthful extravagance from which he would never quite recover. As the years went by, it would make my father sick for anyone even to drive it, to waste the money on gas. So while my mother left her World War II behind, he could not forget his Shanghai. He has brought it with him, and this is where they live.

And so it is she who remains the perpetual traveller, *nicht va?* A foreign person . . . always . . . in a foreign land.

1981

ADOLESCENCE:

Musk

I, the Alien

Summer, 1981, would have been quite dull except for one thing. I'd come home from my freshman year in college having gained . . . a boyfriend.

There was a certain hunched, stunned quality in the way my parents greeted the news.

"So . . . my *putzelinchen* is just nineteen years old—and already there's a young Romeo waiting in the wings?"

"Is he a freshman? Physics major like you?"

"Nope!" I decided to roll it all out right then and there. "He's a musician! A drummer, to be exact. His name is Colin, he's twenty-four, and I'm going to visit him in Pasadena just as soon as you guys let me borrow . . . the car."

"He is a what?"

"A drummer. A blues rock drummer. And not just in his garage. He plays every Tuesday night at the Red Onion with the . . . Jimmy Daniels Blues Band?"

In spite of myself, I'd let my inflection drift up into the question region, as in, "Jimmy Daniels Blues Band? Surely you've heard of them?" Of course they hadn't! These were my parents I was talking to!

Look at their living room: the sad beige couch covered with a floral afghan, the *Scientific Americans*, the Mantovani records. Beyond was my father's blue lounge chair, to which he had tied a head pillow. A head pillow. These were people who could not move ten feet without a head pillow. The neck, the back: everything was starting to go.

These were people who spent every evening at home, reading quietly. Who locked the door behind them when they went to the bathroom in their own house. People for whom the concept of *boyfriend* was some kind of radical teen innovation. These were the space aliens I'd almost forgotten I used to live with!

"I trust your scientific studies have not been suffering with all of this . . . extracurricular activity?"

"Papa: freshman year is all pass/fail! Of *course* I'm doing fine!" As a matter of fact, I'd failed five units of Freshman Chemistry. It was held at the awkward hour of eight in the morning: no one in my dorm got up before eleven.

But my parents didn't need to know that just yet. We had all summer—three long months—to get . . . reacquainted.

What struck me about my parents' house, the first week home, was the sheer silence.

Back in my dorm at school, the pay phone jangled constantly. Freshmen in their pajamas thundered up and down the hall yelling: "Susan, it's for you!" or "Phil—it's your parents!" ZZ Top blared from the stereo; blenders whizzed; sudden squealing broke the air, signaling that freshman Ginny Konikowski was being tickled again.

The yellow wall phone in my parents' kitchen never rang. The only sound you could hear in the afternoons was the ticking of the grandfather clock. Outside the window, geraniums collapsed in the heat. Perhaps a bee buzzed.

I almost jumped when Colin finally called one afternoon.

"Can't talk long. We're cutting a demo. So what's going on, San?"

"Nothing," I racked my brains for something interesting to say. "Except that my parents arc . . . f-f-fucking . . . *space aliens*."

"Know what you mean, man. Mine keep asking me when I'm going to get a 'real job.' "

"So . . . how's the VW?" I hoped against hope.

"Still dead. Transmission. 400 buckaroonis. No can do. Of course, you'd probably know how to fix it, you rocket scientist you."

"Tch . . . Hee-hee-hee-hee! I am not!"

"I swear, I'm waiting for the day when you can support me, you genius girl."

"Tch . . . Hee-hee-hee-hee! I am not! I am not!"

What a misfit I was in this house, I thought when we hung up the phone. I, a person with a drummer boyfriend! I, a person who knew about blues rock! I, a person who could say the word *f-f-fuck* without flinching! "F-f-fuck, this math is hard," I would say all the time at school, or "F-f-fuck, it's hot here!" or "F-f-fuck—I am *so* fucking tired!"

I took a step, twirled, threw out my arms as if to

embrace life. *Kaitlin* sure had never had a boyfriend. She hadn't even gone to her high school prom. I guess fighting with my dad took up all her time.

"What a family! F-f-fuck!" I pushed open the door to my parents' bedroom. This used to be off limits but I was a changed person now. I knew things.

To my right was a king-sized bed with a blue floral bedspread. There was no spot or wrinkle anywhere, just like a hotel. Ahead, a neat teak dresser. Above that, an old brownish linotype of my German grandmother.

Hedwig Jacobsen sat grimly for the camera in a tight bun, a heavy winter coat and black knee socks. She stared at me as though I were something that smelled bad.

"Alien!" I shot back at her. "Alien!"

"At school all of the bathrooms are coed." I was drying dishes with my mother after dinner. "So when you go in, you set the dial to whatever you happen to be: 'Men,' 'Women' or 'Other' . . . Other! Tch! Hee-hee-hee-hee! See? It's a joke!"

"My goodness!"

"Uh-huh. And you should know that I've fallen asleep in guy's rooms sometimes. Oh yeah. We have these crazy study sessions that last 'til one in the morning! Everyone's pretty casual about it, though, it's pretty cool. No big deal."

"So tell me about this musician fellow of yours. This young Romeo, waiting in the wings."

Tch. In my mother's mind, young men always wore tights and leotards and did stag leaps across a stage with bouquets.

On the other hand, she was sincerely trying.

"Okay. Well, like I said, his name is Colin Miller and he's twenty-four years old. Aside from drumming, he's really, really interested in video-making and songwriting. Right now he is recording what is called a *demo tape*. DEMO TAPE. As in, DEMOnstration TAPE. He describes his sound as progressive rock, but politically conscious, with a kind of a 'Yes' feel.''

When I looked back at my mother, she had this kind of glazed expression on her face. She recovered.

"Let me show you something," she murmured. "For when you go see your young man. Something your mother keeps in a secret place."

My mother had a secret place?

We scooted past my father in the living room— *National Geographic*, head pillow—and into the dark hallway beyond.

"Here." She opened the linen closet, reached under the towels and pulled out a glittering glass flask full of this kind of bronze-colored liquid. It had a heavy gold stopper, sinuous designs. It looked like some seventeenth-century relic. Dracula's grail.

" 'Eau de Tatjana.' It's a type of musk. You know what your grandmother always used to say about musk, don't you?"

Grandmother? I couldn't picture that thing in my parents room actually opening its mouth and speaking.

"Musk is never to be worn in public. But *I* think when a young girl goes to see her special young Romeo—just a dab behind the ears!"

"Euuu!"

So that turned out to be the price for my getting to borrow the Buick. Enduring my mother's "secret" musk-spraying ritual. Under the arms, at the neck, behind the ears. Its smell was heavy, old ladyish. A protective coating for young girls.

Although later, as Colin and I stood drinking beers on Chaz the saxophonist's redwood deck, I felt that I at least *looked* cool. I was wearing my black cross-over-the-top Danskin leotard, my cute jeans. (The ones with the zipper up the side? They were really cool.) And I had my hair pulled back, the better to show off my new earrings that Colin had given me—two miniature wooden drum sticks. Really cool.

"It's like when I am playing the drums. I lose all track of time. It's like time itself stops. It is like I'm somewhere beyond time, in a place where—

"Bleeeeaaaaaauuuuuuugh!!!!"

"Oh my God! Are you sick?"

Chaz the saxophonist materialized behind us.

"Hey man. You look really whacked. Why don't you go lie down for a while?"

Colin was dragged, flopping, into the house, but I was not thinking about him anymore. I was thinking about . . . Chaz the saxophonist, with his mane of curly dark hair and eyes that were . . . so blue. Eyes of an older man, in control, at his cool pad that he owned, with a redwood deck and Jeep in the garage. A Jeep that actually worked.

"So Sandy. You want to go in the hot tub?"

"*You* have a hot tub? Oh my God!"

"Sure." He led me to a gazebo in a dark corner

of the yard, pulled back the lid. Inside was a dark, bubbling soup with a bracing piney scent. I was fascinated. I'd never been inside a hot tub before!

"Tch! I just wish I'd brought my f-f-fucking bathing suit."

"Well, it's so dark out, no one will see you. Besides, two ladyfriends of mine are coming later. I don't think they'll—have their bathing suits either."

"Aw, that's all right." But then it came to me. "What am I talking about? I'll just go in in my clothes!

"Oh yeah. We do this kind of thing in college all the time. It's totally f-f-fucking crazy. We have this crazy thing called 'showering' where the freshman are thrown into the showers with all of their clothes on and you get all wet but you laugh and . . . People are pretty casual about it, though. It's pretty cool. No big deal."

I tried to keep my face casual as I slipped my shoes off. I didn't know why these guys were *quite* so amazed. They were musicians, after all. They'd seen a lot, probably more than me! Oh well. Live and let live!

"Ta da!" I kicked out my leg like a chorus line dancer and flopped into the water with a rousing splash!

The next fifteen minutes were the happiest of my whole summer. Chaz lit a candle, which cast a warm orange glow on the water. I sat with them, with the musicians, as they talked their cool musician talk—much complaining about gigs and demos, full of "hips," and "mans," and "cools."

"F-f-fuck yes," I'd say, "f-f-fuck no," and "f-f-fuck . . . maybe." My hair stuck across my forehead; I splashed the water; I was alive!

First there was squealing, then a kind of rustling sound like bushes being crashed through.

"Leeza?" Chaz called out. "Danielle?"

Giggles preceded the appearance of two young

women, a blonde and a brunette, wrapped head to toe in white towels. They stumbled onto the lawn before us, collided into each other, giggled again.

"Ye-e-es!" said the brunette.

"How's the water?" The blonde stuck her head into the gazebo. Her mascara was raccoony. "Any more room in there? Looks pretty tight."

"Pl-l-lenty of room!" said Mickey the guitarist.

"Weeee!" The brunette opened her towel.

I saw the flash of soft rosy breasts, pale naked thighs. Below her tiny delicate—pierced—belly button sprang a dark mass of shockingly curly pubic hair. It was shaved into the form of a—a heart. Behind came the swinging breasts of the blonde. She was wearing only a black g-string and rhinestone ankle bracelet.

"Oh my God," she purred, "this is absolutely delicious!"

But of course, it was Leeza and Danielle who were delicious.

Suddenly my jeans felt tight; my bra pinched; my top slopped heavily against me.

And I realized that I, I was the space alien. I was the thing with bun and black knee socks. It was I who glowered from the portrait in my parents' bedroom. I wasn't cool. I was . . .

But what could I do? It was my DNA. I was a jackalope in dirndl and clogs, raised by . . . Venusians. No matter how hard you tried to hide it, people would always know. You can't escape your genes. Your jeans.

I took a deep breath, rose from the water in all my sopping glory, and sloshed to the stairs.

"I am Sandra," I announced to the earthlings below. "And I'm starting to feel a bit hot. So I take my leave of you all." Why was I speaking so archaically, like my mother? Oh well.

I heaved one heavy thigh over the side, then the other.

"I drove my parents' Buick here tonight," I

added, to make my humiliation even more complete. "They wait for it even as we speak. Adieu!"

It was Chaz the saxophonist who joined me, in his usual Good Samaritan capacity, before I'd gone ten paces.

"Don't worry about Leeza and Danielle. They're nice girls, but a little *trashy*."

Trashy. The word for what I was not.

He leaned forward. Sniffed. "What's that scent you're wearing?"

" 'Eau de Tatjana.' It's a type of musk. My mother made me wear it." I stood there, hair matted, clothes dripping, ego in shreds.

But instead of wrinkling his nose in disgust, Chaz leaned forward and gave me a kiss on the nose. Just like that. Years later, I would remember that gesture as kind. But in that moment, it was wasted on a nineteen-year-old girl who wanted anything but his sympathy.

"Ah, musk. My mother used to wear that! And I always thought it was such an elegant, elegant thing."

Epilogue

Every family picture album, I think, has one photo that seems to sum that family up. I shiver to think what ours would be. But there is one last image I'd like to leave you with.

The year is 1972. The Loh family is in Italy. We've come to see the Leaning Tower of Pisa, a site that satisfies my mother's desire for culture, my father's to deliver yet another science lecture.

"Galileo! He knew that the speed of an object's

fall did not depend on weight. According to the laws of physics, the distance will be related to . . . ?"

Kaitlin looks up from her book. "One . . . half . . . A . . . T . . . squared."

"Yes!"

Giddy with enthusiasm, my father has one last idea. That we, the Loh family, can create a fabulous photographic illusion if we sit in front of the Leaning Tower of Pisa . . . and lean the other way.

"Think how much farther the tower will seem to lean!"

And so, here's how the family photo turns out.

In front: my mother's big brown purse she forgot to remove from the line of vision.

In back: the small, distant Leaning Tower of Pisa.

In front of that: a small Chinese man, two Hispanic-looking girls with Heidi of the Alps braids, and a tall German brunette in Jackie O. sunglasses trying to look very elegant. The only thing binding these four mismatched people is the fact that all are dutifully . . . leaning to one side.

So the photo does not work. The tower does not lean. And, as usual, the Loh family looks as though we're in pain.

On the other hand, who can judge the portrait a family makes?

Who can calculate the ledger of curses versus blessings?

Because what the photo also shows is that . . .

We are in Italy. It's a beautiful day. All around us, the sun shines, the clouds whirl, the breezes fly. And all at once, four travellers sit up and smile, distracted for a moment—like any other family—by the sheer loveliness of their world.

Sugar Plum

Fairy

All I know is one October night in 1976 we changed from ballet people to *Nutcracker* people.

It had been like any other day. My older sister Kaitlin and I had eaten the same after-school snacks (Muenster on pumpernickel, V-8). We'd worn our Thursday leotards (navy and white V-neck, orange skater's skirt). We'd attended our usual classes at the

Mahri School of Dance (Ballet 3 in the big studio, Ballet 2 in the little).

Now my mother was driving us home in the same blue Ford Fairmont. And she was launching into her usual speech.

"Attack, Kaitlin! Attack! That's what your fouetté needs! Attack!"

Kaitlin, hunched and sullen in her parka, said nothing. At sixteen, Kaitlin was "the brilliant one"—hence the one who most often Disappointed. And so she always rode home in the *front* seat, the better to receive this Disappointment. I was always assigned to the darkness and quiet of the *back*, enjoying Vanilla Finger cookies, far from Achievement and its many Complications.

"What is wrong with you? You are like a noodle. Lifeless!"

Kaitlin set her jaw, turned away. "My hamstring—was sore."

"Always with the hamstring! How many more

times are you going to go on about the hamstring? Sometimes I wonder with you, Kaitlin. Do you even want these lessons? Heaven knows it's not cheap. If ballet is just one big chore you should let me know. If getting picked by Irina Lichinska to dance in the *Nutcracker* is not important to you—"

It was the first I'd heard of *this*.

Irina Lichinska was the balletmistress of the famed Los Angeles Junior Ballet. A Russian expatriate, she had a glamorous if shady past: rumor had it, she'd defected from the Bolshoi in the '50s, married a duke, lived in Monaco for ten years. She knew everyone famous at the ABT . . .

Irina Lichinska was the sort of person who could take an average ballet student at the average Mahri School of Dance and lift her up to . . . ?

And the *Nutcracker* was the most glittering spectacle one could imagine. I'd seen its like only in Walt Disney Specials: the candelabra, twisting candy canes, jeweled trees, gingerbread houses, flying walnut boats. Through this Wonderland, girls my age—in full costume and makeup, hair curled and sprayed—threaded their way, faces warmed by the glow of the footlights.

These were the special girls, the Los Angeles Junior Ballet girls. A large, worshipful audience laughed, sighed, broke into applause.

"If getting picked by Irina Lichinska isn't important to you . . ."

My sister turned her Grace Kelly profile, with its upswept bun, back to my mother. "No, it's fine," she closed her eyes tiredly, "I *will* try to . . . work . . . on . . . the fouettés."

"All right, then. Kaitlin."

"What a workout we had in Ballet 2 today!" I exclaimed, from my position way back in Siberia. "Those leaps we did—I practically broke into a sweat! Did you see, Mama? Real sweat!"

My mother glanced back over her shoulder and

tossed me a bone. "Sure, Sandra. Good. You keep trying."

I certainly didn't feel I was a bad dancer. At age thirteen—only three years younger than Kaitlin—I had been studying almost as long as she had did. I was a pretty good jumper and could do the splits.

That's right—the splits. I could sink all the way down. Well, almost all the way down; in truth, I had to cheat a little to the right to get my hips to sit on the floor. But when you looked in the mirror, you saw a person doing the splits.

I imagined Irina Lichinska, elegant in pearls, black cocktail dress and heels, clicking by, tapping a cigarette holder towards me: "I vill take zis one. Look: she can do ze split."

Unlike Kaitlin, I never had a hamstring problem. I loved ballet. I loved what I understood to be the true "dance" part of it—the whirling about the room, mirrors and other dancers spinning around you, kaleidoscopic. I loved the tattered poster of pink satin point shoes in the dressing room: "Ballet . . ." it said, "is Inspiration."

What Kaitlin had going for her, as far as I could see, was good form. Passe, attitude, arabesque: they were clean. She seemed to have almost an obsession with cleanliness.

In warm-ups, other girls would throw themselves into stretching exercises, triple-pirouettes, or other showy endeavors. Kaitlin, by contrast, would stand in front of the mirror and clock through her positions: first, second, third, fourth, fifth. Making the tiniest micro-adjustments. It was almost mathematical, like an engineer tweaking a model airplane.

And her face—totally aloof. (Just that word intrigued me: "aloof." "Aloof," I would sometimes say to myself, winging up one arm and then dropping it like I just didn't care.)

Oh, a "Nutcracker" role would be wasted on Kaitlin. I, I was the true ballet dancer!

It was the day of the audition. The excitement among the sixty dance students crammed into the Mahri School of Dance (with mothers) had reached frenzy pitch. Even the *accessories* were hysterical: tiara-ish *Swan Lake* headbands, chiffon Capezio dance skirts, flashy earrings. One girl had a miniature gold toe shoe hanging from each ear.

Kaitlin's Ballet 3 classmate Darlene Kester, however, had taken it the furthest. Overnight, Darlene Kester's hair had gone from brown to streaky blonde. Not only that, a line of blue pencil and shadow had been applied over each eye! It was Las Vegasy but . . . maybe it would work?

"Irina!" someone called out.

The throng parted, and Irina Lichinska emerged.

In person, the legendary star-maker stood a mere five foot two. Her sixtysomething years on this planet had clearly been tough ones. She had dyed, jet-black hair cut in a lank page boy. She had one rheumy eye; bright red lipstick slashed across her mouth. She wore an oddly mannish trenchcoat and black boots. She looked like a bag lady.

"Hallo! Ai am Irina. Laddees, may Ai entrodeuss Corinna?" From behind Irina stepped a thin-lipped, rail-thin, Audrey Hepburn brunette in a wide cream headband. "She well be ledding your egsersices today: she as expett in Jekady Mathod."

The Cechetti Method? What on earth was that?

The brisk Corinna stepped forward to demonstrate.

"And a one and a two?" Corinna asked, as though it were some deep metaphysical question. She extended her right leg forward.

"And a one and a two," she replied, like that was the whole answer right there, doing a quick relevee on her left leg, beating the right twice at the left knee and whipping it out to the side, her left leg spasming upward into another quick relevee before going into a deft 180-degree pivot.

A taut silence gripped the ragged semi-circle of Mahri School of Dancers. Faces were white. This wasn't ballet, this was . . . algebra.

"All right," Corinna said. "In groups of eight."

Eight stalwart Ballet 3 students stepped forward. The pianist began the intro. *Um pa pa, um pa pa.*

You could feel an audible breath . . .

And then seven girls plunged fatally off in different directions, soldiers falling before the enemy's gun. The Cechetti Method had slayed them.

But one person stood fast. Kaitlin. There she stood in the center, steely as a weathervane, precise as a clock. She was beating the right leg at the left knee, whipping it out, doing a quick relevee, deftly moving into the pivot. Her limbs were chiseled, elegant, clear.

In that moment, I realized that what I couldn't do was *that*. For all my jumping, whirling and half-split, I'd never be able to grasp *that*. *That* was the elusive thing that made one girl stand out from 100. It was Talent, the very Face of Talent.

The question was not which role to give to Kaitlin, but how many. My mother related this in a tumble, as we drove home in the blue Fairmont.

Irina had thought Spanish Princess; Corinna felt they needed Kaitlin to lead the Merlitons. The Flowers too needed help. And how about the Snow Queen? Or maybe even . . . Sugar Plum Fairy.

But Sugar Plum Fairy was an advanced, technical role, usually danced by someone on leave from the ABT.

On the other hand, if done well, it could lead Kaitlin—to New York. In New York was Baryshnikov.

Lincoln Center. My mother went on and on, her voice soaring, cresting, swooping. "Baryshnikov," "Lincoln Center," "New York"—these were words none had ever dared breathe before in the Fairmont.

Kaitlin did not smile, but her face seem to shine in the street lamps that night. New York, I thought. New York. She was really that good.

In short . . .

"How are Kaitlin's fouttés?" had been the blunt question put to my mother.

"Coming along very well, very well indeed" had been her bold reply.

Kaitlin's face contorted into a hideous mask. "Fouttés!" she cried out. "Noooooooooooo! You know that's the one thing I can't do! I always fall backwards!"

But my mother had an answer for everything. A week ago Kaitlin had been a limp noodle: now she was the queen of balletdom, capable of anything.

"All you need," my mother pushed on, "is a little

more attack. That's all. Just like I've been telling you. Look at Darlene Kester. We may laugh at Darlene's blonde hair, and heaven knows she has the flattest feet in the world, but her turns . . . are not bad. She has . . . *attack*."

"Why do I have to be the Sugar Plum Fairy? Why can't I just do the Spanish Dance? Or the Merlitons?"

"We'll work on it at home. We'll do that spotting exercise in the kitchen. Every night."

"Oh noooooooooooooo," Kaitlin repeated, suddenly looking old and tired.

"Are you eating again, Sandra?" my mother turned abruptly.

"Uh . . . yeah," I replied, quickly swallowing my Vanilla Finger. "Just . . . um, just a cookie. Just a couple. I didn't finish them . . ."

"Sandra dear, you need to start thinking about just having a piece of fruit after class. You're getting to be a big girl, quite big. Poor Sandra. Well, your grandmother always said you had good solid legs—legs an empire could stand on."

"What?" I gasped. "What are you saying? I'm big? Do you mean like I'm . . . fat?"

"Spot . . . and spot." My mother's voice drifted in from the kitchen. "Spot . . . and spot."

It was two weeks later. Kaitlin had been training with Corinna by day, drilling with my mother by night. Kaitlin's big fouetté showdown with Irina was tomorrow.

"It's no use," I could hear Kaitlin reply.

"If you'd just have a little more confidence in yourself: Spot . . . and spot. Spot and spot."

I lounged in the dark living room. I was eating peanut butter. I would plunge my finger into the jar, lick. Plunge and lick. Plunge and lick. In twenty minutes, I'd consumed half a jar and felt sick. But what did it matter? I was fat.

On the family scale, under the harsh glare of the fluorescents, I had discovered that I weighed 137 pounds! At age thirteen. It was like a weird dream. How had this grotesque transformation happened?

"Sandra?" I started. Oh, it was just Kaitlin.

"I'm glad you get to be a Flower," she sat down in the darkness with me. "Are you excited?"

"Oh . . . I suppose so. There are, what—twenty-five of us? I just hope they find enough pink tulle in the city to cover us all."

All of us fat girls had been jettisoned into the vegetable kingdom. In the hellish *bolgias*, in the cruel Darwinian pecking order of the *Nutcracker*, only the "Waltz of the Flowers," the lowest rung, would do for us. Any girl who could pull a pair of tights over her hips could be a Flower.

The "Waltz of the Flowers" relied on easy effects you could do with reasonably gifted first-graders.

Open the flowers. Close the flowers. Shake your hands like petals. Turn.

That done, the Flowers' main job was to stand in a semi-circle and look interestedly on while a "ringer"—not a true Flower but a kind of mutant turbo-"Rosette," played by vivacious blonde Darlene Kester—picque-turned about. With that famous *attack* of hers. All this on a slice of grapefruit and a Tab.

"I'm going to be humiliated tomorrow," Kaitlin said suddenly.

"What?"

"No, it's true." I could see her Grace Kelly profile perfectly silhouetted. Her words were said with almost clinical detachment. "My spotting isn't good. Not yet. I think it's because my weight is falling backward on the relevee. It's something I have to relearn. But not in three weeks."

And she was right. After all, she was the genius. She *knew* ballet. She *understood* it.

But one thing Kaitlin was wrong about. She would not humiliate herself the next day.

The pianist began the Sugar Plum Fairy intro as usual. Um plum, um plum, um plum, um plum . . .

On cue, Kaitlin whipped her right leg out and began her painful but impressive hopping-on-one-pointe sequence. She neatly ended the phrase with a deft skip-turn-plié, to murmurs of approval from the throng of watching students and mothers.

"Zat's lavlee, dahling. Lavlee," Irina called out, clapping her wrinkled hands together.

Two short stag leaps done with perfect landings. A general sigh. And then, buoyed by the music, Kaitlin boureed toward the center, the site of the dreaded fouetté sequence . . .

But instead of launching into her turns, that day Kaitlin kept boureeing. And boureeing. Her speed picked up—she broke into a run.

"Dahling?" Irina called out. A murmur arose

from the crowd. The pianist looked nervously over her shoulder—but kept playing.

Because there was no stopping Kaitlin. She kept running about the studio, running—just like in Giselle's mad scene. She was shaking her head no, no, no. And then, giving one final, riveting leap, Kaitlin ran out the door, down the stairs, and caught the bus home.

I didn't have the courage to run from the *Nutcracker*. I stayed, was zipped into my huge pink costume, ate my sandwiches, did my waltz. But I too was changed—because I'd seen that pure steely thing inside Kaitlin. Call it character, call it stubbornness . . .

Whatever it was, it led to the true revelation of my thirteenth year: that a kind of integrity existed that was invisible to the world. That certain acts of courage reaped no earthly rewards. That somewhere in the darkness of the audience my sister sat, bearing her terrible burden, knowing all. Slowly I waltzed with my twenty-four compatriots—our hair curled, our faces rouged—in the bright glare of the foot-lights.

Sandra Tsing Loh is also the author of a novel, *If You Were Here, You'd Be Home by Now*, and a collection of essays, *Depth Takes a Holiday*. She lives in Los Angeles.